MW01251062

PRAYERS FOR MY
Son

by W. Terry Whalin

Other Prayer Books by Terry Whalin

Prayers for My Daughter
Prayers for My Wife
Prayers for My Husband

PRAYERS FOR MY
Son

by W. Terry Whalin

BROADMAN
&HOLMAN
PUBLISHERS

Nashville, Tennessee

© 1999 by W. Terry Whalin
All rights reserved
Printed in the United States of America

0-8054-1854-7

Published by Broadman & Holman Publishers, Nashville, Tennessee
Acquisitions & Development Editor: Vicki Crumpton
Typesetting: Desktop Services, Nashville
Page Design: Anderson-Thomas, Nashville

Dewey Decimal Classification: 242
Subject Heading: PARENTS—PRAYER
Library of Congress Card Catalog Number: 98-54411

Scripture quotations marked NASB are from the New American Standard Bible, ©
the Lockman Foundation, 1960, 1962, 1963, 1968, 1971, 1972, 1973, 1975,
1977, and used by permission; NIV, the Holy Bible, New International Version, ©
1973, 1978, 1984 by International Bible Society; NKJV, the New King James
Version, © 1979, 1980, 1982, Thomas Nelson, Inc., Publishers; and NLT, the Holy
Bible, New Living Translation, © 1996, used by permission of Tyndale House
Publishers, Inc., Wheaton, Illinois 60189, all rights reserved.

Library of Congress Cataloging-in-Publication Data
Whalin, Terry.
    Prayers for my son / by W. Terry Whalin.
        p. cm.
ISBN 0-8054-1854-7 (hardcover)
1. Parents—Prayer-books and devotions—English. 2. Sons—Religious life.
I. Title. II. Series: Whalin, Terry.
BV4845.W433   1999
242'.845—dc21

                                                            98-54411
                                                            CIP

1 2 3 4 5 03 02 01 00 99

CONTENTS

Introduction I

A Prayer for Me *(parent prays for self)* 4

His Attitude 5

His Choices 7

His Education .... IO

His Emotional Makeup I2

His Fears I7

His Future Plans I9

His Health 22

His Honesty and Integrity 24

His Hopes and Dreams 26

His Humility *(includes salvation)* 28

His Love 30

His Obedience 33

His Peace 35

Contents

His Peers 37

His Priorities 38

His Protection 39

His Reputation 40

His Self-Image 41

His Sexual Purity 43

His Speech 45

His Spiritual Growth 47

His Strength 49

His Talents and Abilities 51

His Temptations 52

His Trials 53

His Wisdom 54

His Work 55

About the Author 57

INTRODUCTION

The only Gentile writer in the New Testament, Doctor Luke, told one of the best-known stories about a parent and his sons. Once a father had two sons, and the younger son suddenly demanded his inheritance. "I don't want to wait until you die. I want my money now," this son said.

The father agreed to divide his wealth, and this youngest son packed his belongings and left for a distant land. Soon he wasted his money on wild living, and with no money he began to starve. This boy persuaded a local farmer to let him feed the pigs. As he was throwing food to the pigs, he became hungrier, and the pig food looked delicious. Suddenly, the boy shook his head and came to his senses. He decided that his father's servants had more than enough to eat. He would return home and throw himself on the mercy of his father and become a hired hand.

On the way home, the father spotted his missing son from a distance. This man ran to his son and hugged and kissed him. The son apologized and said, "Dad, I'm no longer worthy to be a son—only a hired hand."

But the father told his servants, "Quick, bring the finest robe in the house and a ring for his finger and sandals for his feet." This father rejoiced in the returned son—he was lost, and now he was found. This story from Jesus is called the parable of the prodigal son.

The story shows the compassion and love of our Heavenly Father toward your son. Whether your son is an infant or in school or starting life on his own, he needs the compassion and love of his parents. One way to give this love and compassion is through consistent prayer.

Through prayer you can ask God to touch your son—yet the results must be left in God's capable hands. He knows the beginning and the end of your days and your son's days. The pages of this book give you a new motivator for prayer. Talking with God, or prayer, isn't like rubbing Aladdin's lamp with wishes. Instead, prayer is your means to communicate with the Creator God of the universe. God invites you to pray for others, and he says in James 5:16, "The earnest prayer of a righteous person has great power and wonderful results" (NLT).

The prayers in this volume are contemporary in style. Speaking to God in prayer is like talking with a best friend about a significant matter. You don't have to use flowery words or specific language; instead, pour out your hopes and plans to this dear friend. These prayers are written in the same style. Each one is a sample to point you in a fresh direction for your prayers related to your son.

Introduction

Prayer doesn't have to occur only in a particular church or place of worship. You can pray at any moment—early or late or during a coffee break or standing in the line at the grocery store. This book is designed to be carried in a briefcase or purse or kept in a desk at the office, then used with spare moments of time.

May God bless the prayers of your heart as you tap into this spiritual resource for your son.

A Prayer for Me

Heavenly Father, I thank you for the opportunity to pray about my son. There is so much to ask for and pray for, yet before I ask you to change this or that, I ask you to touch my own life.

Lord, so often, I don't know what to do or say for my son. I ask you to give me the words that ooze with your love and wisdom. As I pray through these prayers, may the power of your Spirit work in my life and heart. Teach me your ways, O Lord.

Finally, Lord, give me time and energy to pray for my son. Thank you for how you will change me from my time of praying for _____.

Amen.

"And he will give you all you need from day to day if you live for him and make the Kingdom of God your primary concern."

MATTHEW 6:33 NLT

HIS ATTITUDE

God, I pray you will deeply influence my son's attitude. I pray you will help him to set his conversation and mind on the things that are noble, just, pure, lovely, and of good report.

I ask these things with the full understanding that this list of values is often the exact opposite of what he will hear from peers, music, television, and movies. When these other voices crowd into his life and threaten to tear down his spirit and oppress him with the attitude of defeat, I pray in the name of Jesus that you will flood his life with the beauty of your presence. Help my son to understand that he can do all things through Christ who strengthens him.

Amen.

If there is any virtue and if there is anything praiseworthy—meditate on these things.

PHILIPPIANS 4:8B NKJV

His Attitude

Lord God, fill my son with a heart of love for you. I pray that my son will follow you with his whole heart, soul, and mind and in all of his strength.

Father, we acknowledge that it's easy to love ourselves but help _____ to love his neighbor as much as he loves himself.

Fill him with an attitude of love for others. Then people will stop _____ and ask him why he has such an attitude. Fill _____ with your spirit and give him boldness to speak to others about your love—with his words and the attitude of his life.

In the strong name of Jesus, amen.

"And I know it is important to love him with all my heart and all my understanding and all my strength, and to love my neighbors as myself. This is more important than to offer all of the burnt offerings and sacrifices required in the law."

MARK 12:33 NLT

HIS CHOICES

Lord, each new day in my son's life is filled with choices—whether he sees these choices or not. I know that you see the beginning of life and the end of life. As the great author of time and eternity, you see the effects of his choices.

Guard my son's steps today. In a spiritual sense, stand beside my son as he walks through this day and makes small choices. Guide those choices to be the ones that fit into your goals, your dreams, and your plans for my son.

In the name of Jesus, amen.

The old sinful nature loves to do evil, which is just opposite from what the Holy Spirit wants. And the Spirit gives us desires that are opposite from what the sinful nature desires. These two forces are constantly fighting each other, and your choices are never free from this conflict.

GALATIANS 5:17 NLT

His Choices

Heavenly Father, I pray you will guide my son's life today. As my son learns new information, guide that information and help it influence his career choice.

As my son meets new people and crosses paths with friends, use these friends as a positive influence. Help these friends to follow you and your ways.

I pray that you will place a hedge of protection around my son. I know the world is full of evil choices, but I pray that your loving hand will guide my son to make choices that are pleasing to you.

In the mighty name of Jesus, amen.

But the Lord is faithful, who will establish you and guard you from the evil one.

2 THESSALONIANS 3:3 NKJV

His Choices

Lord God, the array of choices my son faces is sometimes over-whelming. Help my son to stay focused on you. When my son makes poor choices, prick his conscience about that choice, then gently guide him to the path of righteousness. If my son makes consistently poor choices, then work in an even more powerful manner to return him to your ways.

Lord, help me not to overdirect his life, but, instead, allow his independence for maturity.

Amen.

"But if you are unwilling to serve the LORD, then choose today whom you will serve. Would you prefer the gods your ancestors served beyond the Euphrates? Or will it be the gods of the Amorites in whose land you now live? But as for me and my family, we will serve the LORD."

JOSHUA 24:15 NLT

HIS EDUCATION

Father, my son learns from a variety of sources. Yet when it comes to formal education in the classroom, most of my son's instructions come from his teachers. I pray for _____, the teacher in my son's life at the moment. As my son almost naturally will admire this teacher, help the teacher to be a person with high moral standards and a good role model.

I don't know where the decisions are made to select my son's teacher. Yet, Father, you stand outside of time and space and know how these decisions are made. Move with your mighty power and guide the selection. Provide these teachers with the proper balance and my son with the right attitude. Thank you in advance for your answer.

Amen.

"A student is not greater than the teacher. But the student who works hard will become like the teacher."

LUKE 6:40 NLT

His Education

Heavenly Father, I pray for my son, _____. I pray you would move in his heart so that he is a person who eagerly thirsts for knowledge and learning. If there are others around him who downplay the teacher or the material, I pray you will give him a supernatural desire to learn the material and to ignore his peers in such pressure.

By the power of your spirit, motivate _____ and help him to learn from the information that crosses his experience. Most important, help _____ to be drawn to your Word, the Bible. Help him to see the divine wisdom in those pages that have transcended centuries of time.

Thank you, Lord, for how you are going to answer this prayer in a manner that is exceedingly and abundantly above all I can ask or think.

Amen.

I saw that wisdom is better than folly, just as light is better than darkness.

ECCLESIASTES 2:13 NIV

Father, you know how on the outside we look like we have it together—yet inside we're broken.

Help _____ to know the depth of your love. If _____ is discouraged, lift his spirit. If _____ feels despair, give him hope.

Lord, many sons are hurting—whether they show it or not. Sometimes their spirits sink so low they believe their only escape is suicide. Place a hedge of protection around my son.

I entrust my son and his emotional makeup into your capable hands.

In the mighty name of Jesus, amen.

But remember that the temptations that come into your life are no different from what others experience. And God is faithful. He will keep the temptation from becoming so strong that you can't stand up against it. When you are tempted, he will show you a way out so that you will not give in to it.

I CORINTHIANS 10:13B NLT

His Emotional Makeup

Lord God, you are the God of all comfort, and you know that my son is discouraged about _____. I pray that my son will not lose heart over this situation, but, instead, learn to cast his cares on you, Lord, because you care for him.

I ask you to undertake the spirit of my son and give him courage in the midst of his discouragement. Give him courage to begin again or head in a completely different direction or seek a new person in a different relationship.

I confess my helplessness for a good answer to this situation in my son's life. Instead, Lord, I turn the entire circumstances over to you and ask for you to direct my son's steps.

In your mighty name, amen.

Be strong, and let your heart take courage,
All you who hope in the LORD.

PSALM 31:24 NASB

His Emotional Makeup

God, I want to begin by thanking you for the variety of human emotions in my son. During his life I've seen the whole range—from great joy and excitement to a deep sadness or depression.

Right now, God, my son is feeling the low side of emotions or depression. I ask for you to surround my son with your loving presence. Strengthen my son in his inner man and help him discover his joy in you. Draw my son close to your words in the Bible, and help those words give him understanding and strength for his circumstances in this day.

Amen.

As pressure and stress bear down on me,
  I find joy in your commands.
Your decrees are always fair;
  help me to understand them, that I may live.

PSALM 119:143–44 NLT

His Emotional Makeup

God, I pray you will lead my son into the truth. I pray that
_____ knows without a doubt that where envy and self-seeking exist,
confusion and every evil thing will be there. I pray in the name of Jesus
that my son will know your wisdom, which is pure, then peaceable,
gentle, willing to yield, and full of mercy and good fruits.

Finally, when he is emotionally upset, teach him how the fruit of
the righteous is sown in peace by those who make peace. Turn my son
into a peacemaker.

Amen.

*For wherever there is jealousy and selfish ambition, there you will find disorder and
every kind of evil. But the wisdom that comes from heaven is first of all pure. It is
also peace loving, gentle at all times, and willing to yield to others. It is full of mercy
and good deeds. It shows no partiality and is always sincere.*

JAMES 3:16–17 NLT

His Emotional Makeup

Lord God, I've noticed my son seems to be feeling sad. In the Bible, I know that a number of key figures like Moses, David, and Jesus were sad at times, yet they came through these sad times with joy.

I pray you will help this time to be one of deep growth in _____'s life. Teach him to cast his cares on you because you care for him. Surround him with the force of your love during this season of sadness.

Help _____ to deal with his sadness in quiet confidence that you will bring joy back into his life. I claim this forthcoming joy by faith and in the name of Jesus.

Amen.

"When you pass through the waters,
  I will be with you;
And through the rivers,
  they shall not overflow you.
When you walk through the fire,
  you shall not be burned,
Nor shall the flame scorch you."

ISAIAH 43:2 NKJV

HIS FEARS

Lord, you are the God of all comfort and peace. I pray your truth will fill my son's life and he will not be afraid.

I ask that when fears come into his life, he will turn from those fears and put his trust in your capable hands. In those times of fear, I pray he will recall the words the apostle Paul wrote to Timothy saying, "God has not given us a spirit of fear but of power and love and discipline." Mold those words into _____'s life.

Amen.

Such love has no fear because perfect love expels all fear. If we are afraid, it is for fear of judgment, and this shows that his love has not been perfected in us.

I JOHN 4:18 NLT

His Fears

God, I pray that you will teach my son about righteousness and help him to live an upright life. As you firmly establish his life in you and a confidence in you, I pray you will remove the force of fear and oppression from _____.

Because of my son's confidence in you and the power of your Word and watchful care, keep him away from terror so it will not come near his life. Thank you in advance for your loving care and concern.

Amen.

Do not be afraid of sudden terror,
Nor of trouble from the wicked when it comes;
For the LORD will be your confidence,
And will keep your foot from being caught.

PROVERBS 3:25–26 NKJV

His Future Plans

Lord, I pray for my son's future plans. First, I ask that _____ would become like King David, a man after your own heart. Bless my son's plans, dreams, and desires.

Guide my son into the profession or career that you have for him. Give him the ability to make an impact and make a difference in his world because of his training and chosen profession.

I thank you that we can make plans and have dreams, but only you, Lord, can see the beginning and the end of my son's life. Direct his steps today.

Amen.

I pray that your hearts will be flooded with light so that you can understand the wonderful future he has promised to those he called. I want you to realize what a rich and glorious inheritance he has given to his people.

EPHESIANS 1:18 NLT

His Future Plans

Lord, as I think about my son, _____, I pray you will direct his steps today. Guide those steps toward your plans for his life. When my son is in the classroom today, guide and work through his teachers. Thank you for the impact these teachers can have on my son's future.

As you direct my son's future plans, bring people into his life who will influence him to godly living—not necessarily that my son will go into a full-time spiritual profession (yet if that is your will, I support it), but that he will see his career as a calling from you.

Thank you, Lord, in advance for how you are interested in the intimate details of our lives.

Amen.

"For I know the plans that I have for you," declares the LORD, "plans for welfare and not for calamity to give you a future and a hope."

JEREMIAH 29:11 NASB

His Future Plans

Heavenly Father, today I want to pray about my son's future wife. As my son dates, surround him with your protection. Give him a consciousness about the sanctity of marriage. Lord, use me as an influence in my son's life—not to nag, but to be a good example.

Then, as my son spends more time with one woman, give my son wisdom in his relationship. If this young woman doesn't know you personally, Lord, then bring her into a relationship with you.

Assist my son and the young woman to set firm boundaries in their physical relationship. Also foster and nurture their emotional and spiritual relationship.

Thank you in advance for your loving hand in this process.

Amen.

He who finds a wife finds a good thing.
And obtains favor from the LORD.

PROVERBS 18:22 NASB

His Health

Father God, thank you for creating my son, _____. I admit that often I take my son's health for granted.

I pray you will give my son health today. Place a wall around him that will shield him from disease and illness. Also, Lord, grant my son good emotional health. Give him a sense of your love and kindness throughout today. Purify his thoughts and give him strength to have emotional balance in his life.

Finally, God, give my son spiritual health today. Provide the inner fortitude so that he draws his values and strength from you and the Bible.

Thank you in advance for answering my prayer.

Amen.

Don't be impressed with your own wisdom. Instead, fear the LORD and turn your back on evil. Then you will gain renewed health and vitality.

PROVERBS 3:7–8 NLT

His Health

Father God, thank you for your deep love for my son, which is far beyond my capacity, though I love him very much.

In my son's sickness, I pray you will touch his life and heal him. Lord, when Jesus walked the earth, he healed the people with various diseases. Now my son needs a touch of your healing hand, and I ask for your help in the name of Jesus Christ.

I pray you will give the doctors divine wisdom about the proper medication and treatment plan.

Finally, preserve my son's life. Lord, I commit my son into your loving hands.

Amen.

Then they cried out to the LORD in their trouble,
And He saved them out of their distresses.
He sent His word and healed them,
And delivered them from their destructions.

PSALM 107:19–20 NKJV

HIS HONESTY AND INTEGRITY

God, in today's world a man of honesty and integrity is rare. The encouragement to cheat and stretch the truth is everywhere.

I pray you will give my son a consciousness of the presence of your Spirit. Then when temptations come, remind him of your Words and give him the strength to live a godly life.

My son's stance on honesty and integrity goes against the tide of the world. I pray you will make him like a tree planted by living water that is deeply rooted in nourishment from you and your truth.

Hold _____ close so he lives with honesty and integrity—today and in the future.

In the name of the Alpha and Omega, Jesus Christ, amen.

Better is a poor man who walks in his integrity
Than he who is perverse in speech and is a fool.

PROVERBS 19:1 NASB

His Honesty and Integrity

Heavenly Father, I want to ask you to quiet the voices of doubt and temptation that will speak to my son today. Not literal voices, but the inner speech that passes through my son's mind and heart—the words that say things like, "It's OK. No one will know." Or, "Just this once, and besides, everyone else is doing it."

Give my son a commitment to godly living and a lifestyle that is pleasing to you. I pray today that you will provide my son with the strength and moral fortitude to resist going along with the crowd.

Give my son the whole armor of God to withstand the evil of the day. Thank you, Lord, for your provision to help my son live with honesty and integrity.

Amen.

"And you will know the truth, and the truth will set you free."

JOHN 8:32 NLT

HIS HOPES AND DREAMS

God, I have hopes and dreams for my son, yet help me not to force those desires on his life. Father, some people don't even try to live up to their potential. Help my son reach for his potential.

I pray you will direct the events and circumstances in my son's life. Use these events to give my son a hope for his future.

Also, awaken in my son the desire to accomplish his dreams. Grant him the persistence to pursue his dreams. Thank you in advance for your leadership in my son's life.

In the name of Jesus, amen.

"For I know the plans I have for you," says the LORD. "They are plans for good and not for disaster, to give you a future and a hope."

JEREMIAH 29:11 NLT

His Hopes and Dreams

Father, there are many things in life that cause discouragement, such as rejection or failure.

When my son, _____, faces these elements of life, I pray you will encourage his heart. Give him the persistence and the patience to continue in the midst of rejection and roadblocks. I pray you will restore hope in his life.

As my son's hope is renewed, use that encouragement to motivate him for the tasks of each day. I pray he will again have dreams and desires for his future.

Lord, you direct the planets in their movement, yet you are interested in the details of our lives. Thank you for restoring the hopes and dreams in my son's life.

Amen.

Hope deferred makes the heart sick,
  but a longing fulfilled is a tree of life.

PROVERBS 13:12 NIV

His Humility

Father, I pray my son will never forget who is the source of success and life itself—you. The Scriptures tell us, Lord, that pride comes before destruction. The proud spirit is the exact opposite of humility. I ask for you to help my son to live with a humble spirit and not pride. Give him the proper balance between a good self-image and humility.

Lord, I also ask you to bring into my son's life people who will speak the truth in love. These friends or loved ones will help my son guard against pride with their honesty and guidance in his life. Give him the ears to hear the loving instruction from these family members or friends. Then help my son to live in humility before you.

Amen.

Pride ends in humiliation, while humility brings honor.

Proverbs 29:23 NLT

His Humility

God, I have to admit that I see my son through rose-colored glasses. When someone tells me something wrong about my son, I instantly rally to his defense, "Why, not _____!" Or if my son gets into trouble, I always listen to his side of the story; then I often defend him.

Today help me see my son with honesty. Also, bring into my son's life people who will see him as he really is. Teach my son to live with a humble spirit.

I ask for you, the Great Teacher, to help my son live in humility. Amen.

He gives us more and more strength to stand against such evil desires. As the Scriptures say, "God sets himself against the proud, but he shows favor to the humble."

JAMES 4:6 NLT

HIS LOVE

Father God, I pray that you will inhabit my son's heart through faith. And I pray my son will be rooted and grounded in your love. As this happens, I pray my son will join the other believers and begin to comprehend the width and length and depth and height—to know your love, which surpasses all knowledge.

I pray my son _____ will be filled with all knowledge of the fullness of God.

Amen.

Now to Him who is able to do exceeding abundantly beyond all that we ask or think, according to the power that works within us, to Him be the glory in the church and in Christ Jesus to all generations forever and ever. Amen.

EPHESIANS 3:20–21 NASB

His Love

Lord God, I admit the world is full of wrong ideas about love. Instead of seeking self-pleasure, teach my son how to love anyone in his path, regardless of whether he receives love in return. Thank you, Father, for the example of Jesus—who laid down his life for all of humanity and called us friends. Help that sacrificial love to drive my son's actions and thoughts. Give my son the ability to show true love to his friends.

I pray my son never forgets your great love, O God, and how you demonstrated it in that while we were yet sinners, Christ died for my son. Protect my son's heart and help him carry that love to others.

Amen.

"Greater love has no one than this, that he lay down his life for his friends. You are my friends if you do what I command."

JOHN 15:13–14 NIV

His Love

God, today give my son a sensitive heart to people. In our world filled with pain, it's pretty easy to develop a thick skin. Instead, provide my son with a sensitive spirit and give him the physical resources to assist the hurting—even to lend a listening ear or a helping hand.

Finally, help my son to care about people—not only for the moment but for their eternal destiny as well. Make my son a prayer warrior for his peers, his family, and his neighbors. Also give my son the boldness to talk about you; then eternally bless his efforts.

Amen.

The man answered, "You must love the Lord your God with all your heart, all your soul, all your strength, and all your mind." And, "Love your neighbor as yourself." "Right!" Jesus told him. "Do this and you will live!"

LUKE 10:27–28 NLT

HIS OBEDIENCE

Father, you say in the Bible that if we have iniquity in our hearts you will not hear our prayers (Ps. 66:18). I want you to hear my prayers for my son. Please reveal if there is any sin in my heart against my son, then give me the strength to correct that matter. I confess that area as sin and ask for your forgiveness.

For my son, _____, I ask you to awake a desire in him to live in obedience to you and your ways. Help _____ take every thought and action under your control. Teach him to embrace the stretching pain of discipline.

In the mighty name of Jesus, amen.

"But I gave them this command: Obey me, and I will be your God and you will be my people. Walk in all the ways I command you, that it may go well with you."

JEREMIAH 7:23 NIV

His Obedience

God, I thank you for the gift of my son.

I pray that you, Father, will be the teacher in my life and help me to teach obedience to my son. Many people get their idea of God from their parents, and I take this role quite seriously. Help my son to know that you are not a policeman with a stick, but you are a loving Heavenly Father who sets boundaries in our lives. Help me to set boundaries of love and discipline.

Amen.

My child, never forget the things I have taught you. Store my commands in your heart, for they will give you a long and satisfying life. Never let loyalty and kindness get away from you! Wear them like a necklace; write them deep within your heart.

PROVERBS 3:1–3 NLT

HIS PEACE

Heavenly Father, my son's world is full of stress and turmoil—at times it seems to come from all corners of life. In the midst of this turmoil, I pray you will teach my son to rest in your peace.

You tell us in the Bible that we should call to you, and you will answer us and show us great and mighty things we have not known. I pray your peace will fill my son's life today. Fill my son so he will be a witness of your grace and love to others with whom he comes into contact today.

If my son has anxiety, help him to throw those feelings on you because you care for _____. Thank you that Jesus can carry his burdens.

Amen.

You will keep in perfect peace
him whose mind is steadfast,
because he trusts in you.

ISAIAH 26:3 NIV

His Peace

Father, I want to acknowledge that the world is becoming more violent. As my son lives in this world, I pray he will be an agent of peace. Give him the supernatural ability to speak words of wisdom from you and to calm potentially violent situations.

I understand the difficulty of remaining calm when chaos erupts. I pray you will give my son a supernatural measure of this ability to promote calmness in the midst of uncertainty.

Lord, you told the people, "Blessed are the peacemakers, for they will be called sons of God." Through peace, help my son be a son of God.

Amen.

But the wisdom that comes from heaven is first of all pure. It is also peace loving, gentle at all times, and willing to yield to others. It is full of mercy and good deeds. It shows no partiality and is always sincere.

JAMES 3:17 NLT

HIS PEERS

Lord of heaven, I know my son's friends influence him. I ask for your blessing on those peer relationships.

I pray for you to direct my son as he selects friends. Work in my son's heart and in the hearts of these friends. Draw my son to peers who have a relationship with you, God. Give my son a loyalty to these friends, and also help these friends to be loyal to my son.

I understand that friends have ups and downs, highs and lows. Help my son to understand this dynamic of friendship and to weather these storms of a relationship in love.

Lord, I thank you for your intimate love for my son and his friends.

Amen.

There are "friends" who destroy each other, but a real friend sticks closer than a brother.

PROVERBS 18:24 NLT

HIS PRIORITIES

God, I recognize your lordship over my son's life. Help my son to seek you first every day. Show my son how to prioritize his life so that only those things with lasting purpose will occupy his time.

Give my son the ability to choose a simple schedule that will allow time with you in prayer. As my son submits his priorities into your hands and seeks you first, I know all of the other details will fall into place. Thank you, Lord, before it happens, for your guiding hand on my son's life.

Amen.

"No one can serve two masters. Either he will hate the one and love the other, or he will be devoted to the one and despise the other. You cannot serve both God and Money."

MATTHEW 6:24 NIV

His Protection

Father God, I recognize these are uncertain times. If I stop to think about it, there is a risk every time my son crosses the street or rides in a car, yet I commit the protection of my son into your capable hands.

Surround my son today with your presence and your love. As he goes through the day, help him to be mindful of you and how you are involved in every detail of his life. I pray you guide the things my son will see today and protect his heart so it stays pure and kind.

Thank you in advance for how you will protect my son from evil today.

In the strong name of Jesus, amen.

But the Lord is faithful, and he will strengthen and protect you from the evil one.

2 Thessalonians 3:3 niv

HIS REPUTATION

Father God, I pray _____ will have a reputation that is untarnished. I pray my son will have the respect of others, and there will never be any reason for people to speak badly of him. Keep _____ free from any legal entanglements. Deliver him from his enemies and defend him from those who would harm him.

I pray my son will bear good fruit and be known from his good actions. May the fruit of trustworthiness and honesty and humility sweeten all his dealings so his reputation will never be spoiled.

Keep my son safe from evil gossiping mouths. Lead my son and guide him each hour.

Amen.

Don't let me be disgraced, O Lord,
  for I call out to you for help.
Let the wicked be disgraced;
  let them lie silent in the grave.
May their lying lips be silenced—
  those proud and arrogant lips that accuse the godly.

Psalm 31:17–18 NLT

HIS SELF-IMAGE

Heavenly Father, help my son to find his identity in you. Give him the ability to define his worth through your eyes and not from the world's standard. I pray you will give my son divine insight about his abilities so he can appreciate that these skills come from your creative hand.

As other voices crowd into my son's life, give him ears to hear you and your Word. Fill my son's heart with peace about your constant love and acceptance. Free him from self-consciousness and self-focus, which can make him feel imprisoned. Instead, allow my son to celebrate your work in his life.

Amen.

For God knew his people in advance, and he chose them to become like his Son, so that his Son would be the firstborn, with many brothers and sisters.

ROMANS 8:29 NLT

His Self-Image

Lord God, my son hears so many mixed messages, which are often negative about him. Fill my son with self-confidence.

Help my son to have a healthy awareness about proper nutrition and diet as well as his physical appearance. Also give him the grace to accept whatever he can't change and the insight to know the difference.

Amen.

For if anyone is a hearer of the word and not a doer, he is like a man who looks at his natural face in a mirror; for once he has looked at himself and gone away, he has immediately forgotten what kind of person he was. But one who looks intently at the perfect law, the law of liberty, and abides by it, not having become a forgetful hearer but an effectual doer, this man shall be blessed in what he does.

JAMES 1:23–25 NASB

HIS SEXUAL PURITY

Father, I ask for a wall of protection around my son today—his body, his spirit, and his mind. The images and encouragement to be sexually impure are everywhere. Give my son the strength and the tools from your Word to battle these forces of evil that invade his life.

Through the power of your spirit, close the door to anything illicit or lustful that seeks to enter his life. If anyone or anything comes into his life that tempts him toward infidelity, I pray you will remove this person or thing from his experience. Help my son fill his life and thoughts with you; then use these thoughts to keep my son sexually pure.

In the mighty name of Jesus, amen.

But our bodies were not made for sexual immorality. They were made for the Lord, and the Lord cares about our bodies.

I CORINTHIANS 6:13B NLT

His Sexual Purity

God, give my son the strength and ability to flee immorality when it becomes a threat to his life. Immorality may affect his life through any means, such as media or friends. Give him the moral fortitude to run from this situation—despite the peer pressure to do something different.

Help my son to live each day with the awareness that his body is the temple of your Spirit.

Amen.

Flee from sexual immorality. All other sins a man commits are outside his body, but he who sins sexually sins against his own body. Do you not know that your body is a temple of the Holy Spirit, who is in you, whom you have received from God? You are not your own; you were bought at a price. Therefore honor God with your body.

I Corinthians 6:18–20 NIV

HIS SPEECH

Lord God, I understand the power of words—to heal or to hurt. I pray you will guard the speech of my son. Give him the insight and forethought before speaking to be aware of the power and impact of his speech.

I ask you to guard my son's mouth so he will only speak words that bring life and edify. Help him not to use foul language nor be someone who uses words to destroy. Prevent my son from grumbling or complaining.

The Bible says that if a man wants a long life, he must keep his tongue from evil and his lips from deceit. Fill my son with your love so that his words to others will build up and not tear down.

Amen.

Words from the mouth of a wise man are gracious, while the lips of a fool consume him.

ECCLESIASTES 10:12 NASB

His Speech

Heavenly Father, allow your love to reign supreme in my son's life so his words will not miscommunicate or wound other people. Give my son a respect for other people—regardless of their race or background or position in life. Help my son to speak words of encouragement and to come to an agreement with others without strife.

Let the words of my son's mouth and the meditations of his heart be pleasing in your sight, O Lord.

Amen.

"And I tell you this, that you must give an account on judgment day of every idle word you speak. The words you say now reflect your fate then; either you will be justified by them or you will be condemned."

MATTHEW 12:36–37 NLT

HIS SPIRITUAL GROWTH

Father, I pray you will touch the life of my son and help him to develop into a young man who walks hand in hand with you. Awake in my son a desire for the Bible and help him turn to it daily for spiritual nourishment. When my son strays from your ways, make him quick to seek forgiveness and repentance.

Help my son to live in your presence. As my son walks in your presence, help him to bear evidence of you—love, joy, peace, patience, kindness, goodness, faithfulness, gentleness, and self-control (Gal. 5:22–23).

Thank you for the spiritual growth of my son.

Amen.

As a prisoner for the Lord, then, I urge you to live a life worthy of the calling you have received. Be completely humble and gentle; be patient, bearing with one another in love.

EPHESIANS 4:1–2 NIV

His Spiritual Growth

God, guard my son from an evil and unrepentant heart. Give my son a desire to turn to you daily and to learn from your words in the Bible. Bring into his life people who know you in a powerful way. Help these believers to direct my son's spiritual growth.

When my son slips, help him be quick to forgive and repent. Then fill his life with a sense of awe at your holiness.

Amen.

And when people escape from the wicked ways of the world by learning about our Lord and Savior Jesus Christ and then get tangled up with sin and become its slave again, they are worse off than before.

2 PETER 2:20–22 NLT

HIS STRENGTH

Father, I thank you that true strength comes from your hand. I pray that my son, who is weak, will have your strength today. While it's good to be strong physically, I'm more concerned, Lord, about his mental and emotional strength.

Give him the inner fortitude to resist the pressures of the world and his peers to bend toward ungodliness. Lord, bring my son to the place in his life where he realizes that without God in his life, he is totally helpless—yet with God at his side, his strength will constantly be a surprise to himself and to those around him.

Thank you in advance, Lord, for your provision of strength in my son's life.

Amen.

He gives power to the weak,
And to those who have no might He increases strength.

ISAIAH 40:29 NKJV

His Strength

Father God, one of the symbols you use for strength throughout the Bible is a rock. The rock is solid and immovable; yet it has strength. I pray you will mold the character of my son and help him to stand on your rocklike strength.

On his own, Lord, he's sure to make mistakes and be weak in his character. Instead, give him the desire to follow you and your ways. Strengthen his heart and his mind so he can follow your leading and direction in his life.

I praise you, Lord, as the immovable rock on which my son can always stand.

Amen.

The LORD is my rock, my fortress, and my savior;
my God is my rock, in whom I find protection.
He is my shield, the strength of my salvation, and my stronghold.

PSALM 18:2 NLT

HIS TALENTS AND ABILITIES

God, I want to acknowledge that my son's talents and abilities come from your loving hand. Instead of thanking you for good genes or a gifted teacher, I want to thank you for the God-given talent in my son since his birth.

Give my son the diligence to discover his talent. Sometimes the discovery takes a lot of trial. Open the windows of opportunity so my son can explore different careers and talents. Lord, provide the right person or persons to provide encouragement as he pursues his talent and abilities.

Whatever his profession or career, I pray he will recognize—then use—his God-given talents for you and the good of your kingdom.

Amen.

I wish that all men were as I am. But each man has his own gift from God; one has this gift, another has that.

I CORINTHIANS 7:7 NIV

HIS TEMPTATIONS

Lord God, I pray you will strengthen my son to resist all temptations. Lead him not into temptation but deliver him from all evil, such as pornography, drugs, alcohol, food addictions, gambling, and any type of perversion.

I want to pray especially that you will remove _____ temptation. Make my son strong where he is weak. Thank you that through the blood of Jesus Christ my son can overcome any evil force in his life.

I commit my son's life into your watchful care.

Amen.

But remember that the temptations that come into your life are no different from what others experience. And God is faithful. He will keep the temptation from becoming so strong that you can't stand up against it. When you are tempted, he will show you a way out so that you will not give in to it.

I CORINTHIANS 10:13 NLT

HIS TRIALS

Father God, my son is in a difficult situation. You know the details. I pray in the name of Jesus that you will help him.

I thank you that you didn't come to remove all of the trials of life, but you did come to give us a power outside of our resources. I ask you to give my son the wisdom and strength for this trial.

Give my son endurance to run the race and not give up. Thank you for your constant care.

Amen.

So be truly glad! There is wonderful joy ahead, even though it is necessary for you to endure many trials for a while. These trials are only to test your faith, to show that it is strong and pure. It is being tested as fire tests and purifies gold—and your faith is far more precious to God than mere gold. So if your faith remains strong after being tried by fiery trials, it will bring you much praise and glory and honor on the day when Jesus Christ is revealed to the whole world.

I PETER 1:6–7 NLT

HIS WISDOM

Father, I thank you that we have no wisdom or strength on our own. I recognize that you are the Creator of wisdom. Your word tells us about how wisdom was one of the first things you created.

I ask for you to divinely provide this important trait for my son and his life. Grant him the insight and wisdom, which can only come from your hand. Give my son a deep desire to know you better each day and to study your Word, the Bible, for the truth contained in its pages.

Thank you in advance for the wisdom you are going to provide for my son.

Amen.

A wise son brings joy to his father,
  but a foolish man despises his mother.
Folly delights a man who lacks judgment,
  but a man of understanding keeps a straight course.

PROVERBS 15:20–21 NIV

His Work

Father, many people find their sense of identity and fulfillment from work. Lead my son to the perfect occupation, which will bring financial success. Then my son can provide for his needs and his family.

In the whole scope of my son's life, orchestrate the events of his work. After my son finds a job, I pray you will bless the work of his hands. Give my son diligence, strength, and faith so he will rise above any tendency to laziness; also give my son a sense of balance in his life so he can understand that he doesn't have to overload himself with work for the approval of others.

I commit his work to you.

Amen.

And may the Lord our God show us his approval
  and make our efforts successful.
  Yes, make our efforts successful!

PSALM 90:17 NLT

ABOUT THE AUTHOR

W. Terry Whalin is the author of more than fifty books, including *The Book of Prayers, A Man's Guide to Reaching God.* He has also coauthored many books, including *First Place* and *Lessons from the Pit* (Broadman & Holman), as well as numerous biographies, which include *Chuck Colson* and *Luis Palau.* The former editor at *Decision* and *In Other Words,* Terry is a full-time freelance journalist and lives with his wife, Christine, in Colorado Springs, Colorado. You can learn more about Terry's work at www.terrywhalin.com.